MULTICULTURAL
LITERATURE

A READER'S GUIDE TO
SANDRA CISNEROS'S

The House on Mango Street

ANN ANGEL

Enslow Publishers, Inc.
40 Industrial Road
Box 398
Berkeley Heights, NJ 07922
USA
http://www.enslow.com

Library of Congress Cataloging-in-Publication Data

Angel, Ann, 1952–

A reader's guide to Sandra Cisneros's The house on Mango Street / Ann Angel.

p. cm. — (Multicultural literature)

Includes bibliographical references and index.

Summary: "An introduction to Sandra Cisneros's novel The House on Mango Street for high school students, which includes biographical background on the author, explanations of various literary devices and techniques, and literary criticism for the novice reader"—Provided by publisher.

ISBN-13: 978-0-7660-3167-8

ISBN-10: 0-7660-3167-5

1. Cisneros, Sandra. House on Mango Street—Juvenile literature. 2. Cisneros, Sandra—Juvenile literature. 3. Mexican Americans in literature—Juvenile literature. I. Title.

PS3553.I78H625 2010

813'.54—dc22

2008046500

Printed in the United States of America

112009 Lake Book Manufacturing, Inc., Melrose Park, IL

10 9 8 7 6 5 4 3 2 1

To Our Readers:

We have done our best to make sure all Internet addresses in this book were active and appropriate when we went to press. However, the author and the publisher have no control over and assume no liability for the material available on those Internet sites or on other Web sites they may link to. Any comments or suggestions can be sent by e-mail to comments@enslow.com or to the address on the back cover.

♻ Enslow Publishers, Inc., is committed to printing our books on recycled paper. The paper in every book contains 10% to 30% post-consumer waste (PCW). The cover board on the outside of each book contains 100% PCW. Our goal is to do our part to help young people and the environment too!

Illustration Credits: Andres Balcazar/iStockphoto, p. 8; Associated Press, p. 14; Courtesy of Carolyn S. Shealer, p. 56; Hillery Smith/MCT/Landov, p. 71; Jason Koski, Cornell University Photography, p. 100; Maria L. Antonelli/ Rex USA/courtesy Everett Collection, p. 4; Milbert O. Brown/.MCT/ Landov, p. 83; Milbert O. Brown/MCT/Landov, p. 10; Photos.com/© 2008 Jupiterimages Corporation, p. 7.

Cover Illustration: Jeni Crone.

Contents

5   CHAPTER 1: Tug of War

27   CHAPTER 2: Plot and the Experimental
Structure of Vignettes

39   CHAPTER 3: Themes of Embracing Culture
and Pushing It Away

49   CHAPTER 4: Poetic Devices

55   CHAPTER 5: The Character of Esperanza
Cordero

59   CHAPTER 6: The Corderos' World—Culture,
Class, and Stereotypes

63   CHAPTER 7: Other Works

85   CHAPTER 8: The Importance of This Work

100   CHAPTER 9: Best-Seller Lists and Awards

❋

109   CHRONOLOGY

111   CHAPTER NOTES

121   GLOSSARY

122   MAJOR WORKS BY SANDRA CISNEROS

123   FURTHER READING

124   INTERNET ADDRESSES

125   INDEX

128   ABOUT THE AUTHOR

Sandra Cisneros

CHAPTER 1

Tug of War

As a child living in Chicago's Humboldt Park, Sandra Cisneros remained blissfully unaware of the difficult lives of Mexican Americans and, especially, the lives of Mexican–American women. That does not mean this only daughter in a family of six brothers lived an idyllic existence. Sandra, born of a Mexican father who spoke Spanish and a Mexican–American mother whose primary language was English, grew up in a family that lived in a working-class neighborhood, with parents who believed they were better than their circumstances. Their roots ran long, all the way to Mexico where Sandra's grandparents still resided. Each summer, the family stored their furniture, loaded coolers with bologna sandwiches for the journey, and packed their station wagon with a summer's worth of belongings for their pilgrimage to Mexico to visit grandparents, cousins, aunts, and uncles.

*

They returned to Chicago each fall where the family would take furniture out of storage and relocate in the Humboldt Park neighborhood to a new apartment. The frequent moves created a sense of "temporary existence," or impermanence, in Sandra's life. This same sense of impermanence is captured in *The House on Mango Street,* where Esperanza Cordoza's desire for a house all her own symbolizes the accompanying struggle to find out how ethnicity and gender shape her identity.

Through the process of seeking this special house—a place that can be a true home—Esperanza explores the elements of her neighborhood, a neighborhood that proves to include elements that are inhospitable, in a search for self-esteem and identity. This struggle mirrors Sandra's experience growing up in a community that failed to cherish some of its members. While her parents

Sandra Cisneros was born and raised in the city of Chicago in Illinois.

encouraged their seven children to be better than their surroundings, others in the community treated those of different cultural and economic

The Cisneros family would travel to Mexico City (above) each summer to visit their relatives. They split their lives between two cities, which, on the outside, look very similar. Culturally, however, they were very different. The young Sandra Cisneros felt like she did not completely belong to either Mexican or American society.

backgrounds with disdain. "Teachers didn't always treat us as if we were anything special," she explains about the way school proved to be one of the most difficult places to fit or feel special as a child. A product of Catholic schools, Sandra recalls her reaction to the unkind way some teachers treated her and other children. "They really turned me off to spirituality," Sandra says. "The nuns were very mean to the poorer children, which meant Mexican children." But her family's values proved stronger than the rejection she experienced. "Even though we weren't loved at school, our mother and father loved us a great deal and they had such great faith and love in us that, even though we were buffeted by circumstances beyond our control, we had that core of self-esteem that our mother and father had given us. . . . I think that's why I've been able to survive the neighborhood I grew up in, the institutions I went to."[1]

Sandra was a shy, quiet student who often brought home a report card full of Cs and Ds. She believes the report cards reflected her teachers' inability to understand what it meant to be a working-class, Mexican-American girl from Chicago. "They thought I was a dreamer," she

Cisneros holds up a family picture. Her mother, Elvira, is standing on the left. Although there was very little respect for the children at school and not a lot of money in their bank accounts, the one thing the Cisneros family had a great abundance of was love for one another.

says. The petite, dark-haired woman, who easily flashes smiles and uses her lyrical voice to disarm her audiences, describes her less-than-perfect adolescence: "I was the girl in the corner with the goofy glasses from Sears. I was the ugly kid in the class with the bad haircut, the one nobody would talk to. I was the one that never got picked to be in the play."[2]

Cisneros's father, a Mexican national—an upholsterer, whose first language was Spanish—became a naturalized United States citizen as a benefit of serving in the military during World War II. He was one of the many immigrants who crossed the border to find work.[3] A large Mexican community grew in Chicago as a result of the railroad. During the fifties, many Mexicans came north through the railroad lines for industrial jobs. Nevertheless, Cisneros says her Humboldt Park neighborhood included many other nationalities. "I grew up with Ukrainian girls, Polish girls, African-American girls. . . . I just thought that was how the world [was] and I was right; that is how the world is."[4]

Still there are pockets of prejudice and those influenced Sandra as a child and continue to influence her now. It is the autobiographical influence of this life that is captured in vignettes of adolescent Esperanza, the fictional main character in *The House on Mango Street.* "The way we grow old is kind of like a tree trunk, all the rings are inside the other, and I feel that way. I'm 36 on the outside, but inside I'm also 11, and 5. It's real easy for me to write from the perspective of all the characters I wrote about because I don't forget what it felt like. I don't think as artists we let those memories go. They're inside us." Esperanza, then, is in many ways the ring inside the trunk that represents the eleventh or twelfth year of Cisneros's life.[5]

"People take what I write as autobiography," Cisneros has noted. But while her work might begin with a memory, she uses pieces of other people's stories. She often tells the story of how, in fifth grade, she was searching the card catalog in the library and came across a dirty and bedraggled book card. She realized this book had been read by a lot of people and she wanted it to be her card. Then she visualized her name on the spine of a book. But she kept the image to herself.

Wanting to write was absurd in her neighborhood. She says she believed, "it was as absurd as wanting to be a witch."[6]

While in grade school and even for most of high school, Sandra did not tell people about her writing. "I kinda did it on the sneak. I think I did it in private because it mattered so much to me. School was a place where people destroyed things that mattered to you. At home I had six brothers. Of course I wasn't going to tell them because they would torture me with that. So it was something I kept in a notebook."[7]

While the writer grew up imagining a writer's life, her family had more traditional plans for her. Sandra's father wanted her to go to college, but Cisneros says, he "only meant for me to go to college to meet a nice educated young man. When I finished my undergraduate at Loyola and I didn't have an engagement ring, he was sort of worried about me."[8]

After college, the desire to write still captivated Cisneros. She applied and was accepted to one of the most prestigious writing programs in the United States: the University of Iowa Writers Workshop. "I was told it was the place to go," she says. But the experience of suddenly finding herself in a workshop setting with mostly upper-middle-class white men was difficult for her as well as the other women and people of other

Cisneros entered the University of Iowa Writers' Workshop to complete a master's degree in creative writing. The program is housed in this mid-nineteenth-century mansion known as the Dey House (above).

cultures who attended the elite program. They were the silent participants who kept to the fringes of the groups. She found herself afraid to join in discussions and sat in the back of the room with another poet, Joy Harjo, a single mother with whom she remains close friends today. "When we did say something, people would look at us like we were from Mars." Later on, Cisneros learned that poet Rita Dove, who was a fellow student, worked up all her courage so that each day she could offer a single comment in such intimidating conditions.[9]

Harjo and Cisneros became each other's anchors in the early workshop, reading each other's work and keeping each other in the program. "If I hadn't met Joy when I did, I would have quit the workshop," says Cisneros of the class where she began work on Esperanza's story.[10] The story came to her one day when Cisneros was sitting in a workshop listening to the other students talk about their houses, their homes. She could not quite relate because these were not the houses of her growing experience and they certainly did not reflect the spaces that she perceived would make a home. But when Cisneros tried to tell of her own houses, no one understood. The significance of her stories about wanting a home was lost on these students. "When I said something in class, there would be absolute silence," she says. She quickly realized that she needed to figure out what she could do to survive in the classroom and push forward. In these workshops, she felt the silence of racism against her as a Latino and she did not know how to find her own voice. This was the racism that she realized most outsiders to a group experience, but she was not sure what to call it then. "The thing about racism is that it's so subtle that you don't have a name for it until after it's happened. . . . When it's happening to you, you're powerless unless you can name it."[11]

Once she understood the experience, Cisneros says it filled her with "couraje," a combination of rage and courage. She explains, "The thing about rage is it also gives you courage if you don't use it against yourself."[12] So Cisneros decided she would write to create her world, the opposite of what the more privileged students were writing. If they wrote of large suburban homes with lush furniture, she would write about the houses of her childhood. If the other students used language that was effusive and academic, she would turn simple language into poetry. Her work was immediately recognized for the fresh and individual voice and, whether she was working on Esperanza's story or her poetry, it started to gain the attention of publishers.

"Mexican Hat Dance" was Cisneros's first poem. She sold the poem to *Nuestro* magazine, which she describes as "sort of like the brown *Ebony*."[13] The magazine is defunct now and

Cisneros acknowledges that she never got paid for the poem.

Bad Boys, a chapbook of six poems that were part of her thesis at the University of Iowa and part of a series of chapbooks published by authors Gary Soto and Lorna Dee Cervantes, was produced in 1978, the year Cisneros graduated from Iowa. These chapbooks were staple-bound collections of six to eight poems that were created for audiences who might have heard a poet read her work and could then purchase an affordable copy of the poems.

Cisneros was discovering that her writing was taking on a fight against a patriarchal culture that smothers women's dreams through expectations that they should settle down with a husband and children rather than pursue a career. She also found, through her experience at the Iowa workshops, that the experience of struggle for identity is universal. While only twenty-one years old, Cisneros went to work teaching high-school dropouts. There, she began to translate the Iowa experience of exclusion because of culture and gender, an experience that stayed with Cisneros long after she graduated, into the character of Esperanza. While Cisneros stresses again and again that Esperanza is not autobiographical, this character's struggle reflects Cisneros's own search for identity. She says, "The most autobiographical part of anything I write are the emotions. All the rest is story."[14]

Esperanza also reflects Cisneros's search for what she describes as her own feminism. "If you don't know who you are as a woman, or as an ethnicity, or whatever, you're vulnerable to people telling you who you are." As she searched through Esperanza's developing character, Cisneros discovered the background of her own truths. "I was lucky that I grew up with a very strong sense of self-esteem from my father and from first hand knowledge of Mexico."[15]

But in hearing the stories of her students, Cisneros wanted to capture them, too, in *The House on Mango Street*. "Esperanza's made up of many people," she says. "I wanted her to be an alternative to the lives of my students." Cisneros created this symbolic young woman with a symbolic name, which means "hope" in English.[16]

Cisneros luxuriated in her first opportunity to live alone when she rented a small place near her school and wrote evenings and weekends while teaching. Her father, who believed in and encouraged the family tradition of adult children living with their parents until marriage, could not understand why she needed to be on her own. As much as Cisneros loved her own space, she describes those late nights writing and fighting the way her mind shifted to bouts of loneliness and anxiousness. She would think, as if it were her mantra, "I can live alone and I love to work." She adds that this was an especially difficult transition for her because, "it's hard if you are a Mexican woman and used to living with your family and not estranging them. It was like being a traitor to your country."[17]

Her students were mostly young women who had lives much more difficult than hers had been. Many had parents who discouraged their educations. Others had babies who needed such basics as food and shelter. Some were women who came to school with blackened eyes. Others talked of abuse at the hands of boyfriends and fathers.[18]

But Cisneros was single, and had a loving and supportive family who, while they did not understand why she was compelled to write, did encourage her. She describes the true source of her stories: "People presume because my books seem so realistic that they have to have happened to me. But you have to remember all the things that happen around you, to people you know, or things you witness, or stories people tell you, all the stories that touch you in a day; there are millions of them, and you can borrow them and cut and paste as I do . . . I used a lot from all of the women I know who are unhappy and there are a lot of unhappy women."[19]

Cisneros translated her students' stories of growing up on the margins, exploring budding sexuality, and finding your own identity and place in a world that can be harsh into the stories of Esperanza's neighborhood, her friends, and family. The short vignettes blended to represent Esperanza's search for identity and place.

All the while Cisneros persisted in efforts to complete the novel, her students' lives and their stories and the teaching workload made writing slow. Cisneros realized she needed more time to write. At a point when Cisneros felt she was struggling to find little moments, she was offered a National Endowment of the Arts grant that paid her to live as a writer. This allowed her to travel to Greece where she completed *The House on Mango Street* within one year.

The novel was published by a small publishing company that specialized in Latino writers, Arte Público Press in Houston, Texas, in 1984.

"The important part of writing was to help to heal a community that was in pain," Cisneros says. She takes pride in knowing that she looked around at the world, and when she recognized that the Latin American community, as well as her community of women, was in a state of crisis, she used a pen to help create change. She says, "When I was writing House I didn't know how teaching poetry, and writing poetry, and writing my little stories, was going to change anything and now I see that the stories go out there like notes in a bottle."[20]

That quiet beginning with a small publishing firm has led to an impressive career and the knowledge that she has helped a great many people. Cisneros sometimes receives letters telling her that her stories have touched the hearts of her readers. She describes the joy of knowing that her stories have, in fact, made a difference in the communities she originally wanted to reach. She likes to think of her work as "warning and perhaps guiding people and sometimes giving people permission to express themselves and get by."[21]

Since then, she has received numerous awards and another NEA grant to produce *Caramelo,* a novel that took nine years to write, as well as two volumes of poetry, *My Wicked Wicked Ways* and *Loose Woman;* a bilingual picture book based upon a vignette from *The House on Mango Street,* entitled *Hairs/Pelitos;* and a collection of short stories entitled *Woman Hollering Creek.*

In seeking and finding her own identity through her writing, Cisneros takes great pride in embracing the culture of family, work ethic, and rich traditions in which she grew up. Now she lives and writes in San Antonio, Texas, where she says it

THE CHICANO RENAISSANCE

By 1969, Chicano studies was being offered through English and Social Studies departments at some colleges and universities, and Chicano literature began to reflect a sense of national identity and community. Initially, writers such as poet Octavio Paz wrote about the bicultural world of people who speak both Spanish and English. His writing brought individual stories to readers and broke down stereotypes. By the late 1980s, Chicano authors, including Julia Alvarez and Sandra Cisneros, were being described as "small guerrilla bands" using their stories to help foster a sense of healthy self-identity. These female writers stood up for the women in a culture that forbids females from displaying outrage against their outrageous treatment. Although Cisneros challenged her culture's ideas that women should remain home until they are married, and should respect and obey the men who took charge, she was careful to avoid antagonism from within. "None of us wants to abandon our culture," she said. "We're very Mexican, we're all very Chicanas. Part of being Mexican is that love and affinity we have for our *culture*. We're very family centered, and that family extends to the whole *Raza*. We don't want to be exiled from our people."[22]

For this reason, Cisneros purposely used simple language and short stories in her first novel *The House on Mango Street.* It was written so that everyone who picked it up would be able to read it. The popular work was one of the first novels that reworked American literature to include diverse cultural expression to include diverse literature across the United States.[23]

is important to hear both languages she grew up with. She says she loves the complexity and contrast. "I'm hearing," she explains, "how the two languages are sparking and stretching each other."[24]

CHAPTER 2

Plot and the Experimental Structure of Vignettes

The House on Mango Street began as little poems about a real place remembered. But Cisneros filtered her own memories through the stories of her students—whose lives were so overwhelming she thought they made her life look pampered. "I didn't know what to do about their problems," she says. "I didn't know what to do to save their lives. . . . When they would tell me stories of their lives and cry, I'd cry, too. . . . I think, out of my sense of helplessness, I took those stories and wrote them and I wrote them with all my heart. I didn't write them thinking I wanted to become famous. No ego was involved in writing this book. I wrote it absolutely from my heart."[1]

Cisneros wanted to take her students into her own home and to take care of them and make them go to school. But they had such difficult and different lives. The inability to know how to help stirred questions about how to save one's own life in Cisneros's mind. Esperanza became the narrator who asked the questions that Cisneros was asking herself.[2]

The structure appears, at first, to be a series of simply constructed stories that meander from subject to subject. But the apparent randomness disguises Cisneros's artful exploration of themes that include "individual identity in contrast to communal loyalty, estrangement and loss, escape and return, and the lure of romance set against a dead end of sexual inequality and oppression."[3] Cisneros intended the overall structure of the novel to be one in which the novel tells "one big story, each story contributing to the whole—like beads in a necklace."[4] Trained as a poet, she planned the prose poems, or vignettes, so that readers are able to open the book at any point and read a complete story. But the reader can also begin to read from the first word through to the end to discover another layer of story, one that portrays Esperanza's struggle for identity as a Chicana, a woman and a Mexican American, surrounded by poverty and oppression. In this way, *The House on Mango Street* is a series of interrelated stories that build to this coming-of-age journey and search for identity for Esperanza.

Each vignette is a scene depicting simple moments when Esperanza contemplates her surroundings and her feelings about where she might fit in. The moments might be as simple as Esperanza contemplating the meaning of names, which is the story line in "My Name." Or the moments might be neighborhood scenes such as

"The Family of Little Feet" in which Esperanza and her friends Lucy and Rachel receive a bag of discarded high heels that they try out. Wearing the heels and walking down the sidewalk, the three girls get attention, both positive and negative, and discover what life might be like as adult women. Overall, the stories work together so that each story builds to Esperanza's understanding of who she is.[5]

Just as this novel opens with Esperanza yearning for a house she can call a home, Cisneros recalls from her childhood "a real house and a real emotion of shame." Small vignettes, relying upon simple and poetic language, help her to portray this emotion in the stories of Esperanza's neighborhood. The tiny stories, some as short as a half a page, serve as a collage that layers and shapes Esperanza's experience of belonging but not belonging because she feels cheated out of the house her parents always told her she would get.[6] That would be a house with running water, real stairs, three washrooms, and trees in a large yard.[7] The novel begins with Esperanza arriving at her new house on Mango Street and realizing this is not the house of her dreams. Her disappointment is evident in the way she describes the house:

> But the house on Mango Street is not the way they told it at all. It's small and red with tight steps in front and windows so small you'd think they were holding their breath. Bricks are crumbling in places and the front door is so swollen you have to push hard to get in. There is no front yard, only four little elms the city planted by the curb. Out back is a small garage for the car we don't own yet and a small yard that looks smaller between the two buildings on either side.[8]

Through the reflective stories of her family, neighbors, and friends, Esperanza compares her own sense of being out of place to the way she sees others' lives. We learn in an early vignette, "Boys and Girls," that Esperanza recognizes she and her sister Nenny do not fit into the macho world of their two older brothers. The boys can wander freely in the neighborhood and often take risks. Esperanza sees that this is the way of all the boys in her Chicano neighborhood. In "Louie, His Cousin and His Other Cousin," it even appears that risk sometimes includes breaking the law, when Esperanza discovers the boys have stolen a car for a joyride.[9]

A number of vignettes demonstrate that, while the boys in the neighborhood are free to hang out and to roam, the girls and young women are trapped by their patriarchal, or macho, culture and by their desire to find a man to protect them. Everywhere Esperanza turns she sees young girls and older women waiting for these men to save them. There is Marin, in the vignette of the same name, who waits for her boyfriend in Puerto

Rico to come back and help her escape from this neighborhood. She tells the girls that he will marry her and they will live in a big house far away.[10] Rose Vargas, in "There Was an Old Woman She Had So Many Children She Didn't Know What to Do," is saddled with babies on her hips and children running into streets, making her so tired she cannot keep track of them all.[11] Some of the women look out at the world through tiny windows, trapped in their own little worlds and waiting for their men to return to them. Rafaela is one of these women. Locked into her apartment by her husband on the nights he plays dominoes, she leans on her elbow and dreams while looking out of her window in "Rafaela Drinks Coconut and Papaya Juice on Tuesdays."[12]

Sally, Esperanza's sexually precocious friend, with her black suede shoes and more mature ways, has a mother who rubs lard on the bruises her father has caused. Sally, who appears in a number of the vignettes, is the girl Esperanza desperately wants to be like at first. But Sally frightens Esperanza with the way she goes off with boys. Esperanza feels foolish when she runs to Sally's mother believing the boys are taunting Sally only to learn that Sally likes the attention. On another occasion, Esperanza is molested by a group of boys while she waits for Sally. "Red Clowns," a vignette that captures Esperanza's distress, describes her despair when she accuses Sally of lying to her about how good it feels to be with a boy. Soon after, Sally marries, and Esperanza portrays her in "Linoleum Roses" sitting at home waiting for her husband but afraid to go outside without his permission. Esperanza says, "She has her husband and her house now, her pillowcases and her plates. She says she is in love, but I think she did it to escape."[13]

Esperanza also notices those in her neighborhood who hope for more of life than the neighborhood can offer. There is Minerva who write poems,[14] and Alicia who gets up early to make her father's tortillas, but who also studies at the university in the hope of creating a better life for herself.[15] In "Cathy Queen of Cats," Esperanza befriends a young girl whose family will soon move on to a new neighborhood, a better neighborhood. Esperanza contemplates the many ways she and her family do not fit into the world of Cathy, whose own family will "have to move a little farther north from Mango Street, a little further away every time people like us keep moving in."[16] While Cathy's family feels they must keep moving further and further from these brown-skinned families, Esperanza recognizes that she feels safe in her neighborhood because their brown skin is also hers. Still, she acknowledges that others fear coming into a neighborhood like hers and fear the color of their skin in the vignette "Those Who Don't."[17]

Esperanza is also caught between the world of childhood and her own adulthood, a dilemma that compels her to assess the lives of the adult women she knows. While the men go out into the world, the women's lives have become closed off and limited through their father's control or their marriages. In "A Smart Cookie," Esperanza's mother makes no secret that her own life is narrow and dependent upon her husband. But it is shame that kept her from furthering her education when, despite the fact that she was smart enough to know two languages, she left school because she did not have nice clothes. Esperanza's mother, who used to draw, and who listens to opera and believes she could have been somebody, warns Esperanza to stay in school and make something of her own life.[18] This scene that reveals why she never continued school, but wishes she had, heightens the significance of the girls' struggles to make their lives better, so Esperanza sees hope in the way Alicia studies at the university and in Minerva's poetry.[19] In fact, the way

Minerva shares Esperanza's creative ability, and the way they share their secret writings with one another in "Minerva Writes Poems," is actually the two encouraging one another to find their own voices.[20]

As the vignettes evolve, it is finally through her writing that Esperanza discovers her identity. She sees her writing as a way to escape Mango Street and, in doing so, she also discovers that Mango Street is a part of who she is. The neighborhood's three sisters help Esperanza make the connection when they tell her she must come back for the others. They tell her, "You will always be Esperanza. You will always be Mango Street. You can't erase what you know. You can't erase what you are."[21]

Although she had already published more than thirty poems in literary magazines before publishing this novel, Cisneros received scant notice from large publishers. *The House on Mango*

Street also received little critical attention when it first came out in 1984. Arte de Público, the first publisher of *The House on Mango Street* and the largest publisher of Chicano writers, was, according to Cisneros, not seen as a valid publisher by most Americans. So, while audiences grew through word of mouth, the book received few reviews.[22]

CHAPTER 3

Themes of Embracing Culture and Pushing It Away

Cisneros believes that the weave of cultural themes in the stories in *The House on Mango Street* was influenced by her own grandmothers and great-grandmothers, many who may have been illiterate but who made beautiful cloth. "In order to weave, you have to have a design. Fiction is creating a weave," she says. Cisneros imagined these ancestors weaving the colors in their cloth and realized that the primary weave in Esperanza's life is the story of the house of the imagination; this is the house that Esperanza longs to call a home. Her journey into adulthood became a second design in the weave. Esperanza's discovery that her stories and her writing might be the home inside herself becomes a third weave. This is also the weave in which Esperanza seeks an identity beyond the one portrayed by the poverty and powerlessness of the women in her community. Esperanza does not want to join them to become one of the women locked inside her house, looking out a window, and waiting for her husband.[1]

This search for independence and control becomes evident in the vignette "My Name" when Esperanza contemplates the difficulty of her name, with its many syllables, in the same metaphoric way she considers the difficulty of her life. Difficult to pronounce, there is no nickname and she does not believe it is pretty. This was also the name of a beloved great-grandmother who, forced to marry, always looked out the window sadly and waited for something else in her life. Esperanza perceives it as a name of sadness, a name that does not reflect who she really is. She wishes she could re-baptize herself with a new name, one with a pretty nickname that shows her true self. She imagines herself bearing a name that depicts strength and independence. A name like "Lisandra, Maritza or Zeze the X."[2]

The House on Mango Street includes mythological and fairy-tale elements, influenced by the stories Cisneros loved as a child. These elements enhance the idea that there is magic and power in Esperanza's writing. The oral tradition of those tales "becomes the invented voice and you can hear it a bit in *House*," Cisneros says.[3] While she was influenced by the Brothers Grimm and the characters in the first book she ever owned, *Alice in Wonderland,* characters in the vignettes who resemble these archetypes influence Esperanza's decisions. "It was as if Alice in Wonderland became a cast member of a Mexican telenovella," Cisneros says of the inclusion of these characters.[4]

They include a neighborhood witch, or fortune-teller, who foreshadows Esperanza's future choices. In "Elenita, Cards, Palm Water," Elenita relies on her holy candles, holy water, and Tarot cards to read Esperanza's fortune. When Esperanza asks if the witch can see a house, Elenita responds with the theme of *The House on Mango Street*: "I see a home in the heart."[5] Later, three old sisters from the neighborhood appear as an allusion to the Greek tale of the Triple Goddess, who as three selves entwined as one, signifies the weavers of destiny. They remind Esperanza that she will come back to Mango Street, foreshadowing her destiny and reminding the girl that her story begins on this street.[6]

Issues of ethnic identity, poverty, and other aspects of the Spanish and English bicultural world that Esperanza inhabits unfold through distinct language. Cisneros acknowledges, "I wasn't even aware that my first book, *The House on*

Mango Street, was so influenced by Spanish until I finished the book." But she wants her writing to reflect that, although readers might be reading English, the characters are speaking Spanish. In the rhythms and cadences of immigrant voices, Cisneros uses language to open windows to other worlds, to invite readers in to a bilingual, bicultural world. Words and syntax mimic the patterns of Spanish language. Cisneros says this allows readers to see something of themselves in people they might not initially perceive to be alike. "The magic and power of a story is it will allow you to be transported from this environment and take you to another. It's speaking to some great emotional need that we have and those are the stories that speak to us and that we listen to. They touch our hearts."[7]

While Esperanza speaks with neighbors and friends, Cisneros chose not to put these conversations in quotation marks. This was an intentional choice of the trained poet who believes that punctuation can serve the writer's needs on many levels. When she tried the text with quotation marks, she felt the manuscript looked peppered with punctuation. By removing quotations, Cisneros liked the way conversations serve a dual purpose, or a simultaneous role, as exposition and dialogue. Cisneros describes this technique as "an experimental way to make the sentences bend."[8]

Esperanza's story is told in language that seems simple and straightforward, relying on some slang and shifts from grammatical correctness to reflect the speaking patterns of Esperanza's neighborhood, but, "in that simplicity, it possesses the richness of poetry," to capture the immediacy of the poor Chicago neighborhood that is Esperanza's.[9]

Cisneros revised many times to attain Esperanza's simple, poetic voice. The choice of language, the punctuation, the simplicity of language, and the way vignettes fall together to create a story within a story were all deliberate choices, made with an eye toward art. "When you make art," Cisneros says, "you have to shape something so it's perfect with a beginning, a middle and an end."[10]

The tension between the two languages of Spanish and English in *The House on Mango Street* develops the conflict between Esperanza's struggles of individuality versus community, as well as the struggle between two cultures. Esperanza sees the women in her community confined by their culture, their poverty, and their men. Her neighbors are confined, or locked, inside their houses as in the scene in "Rafaela Who Drinks Coconut and Papaya Juice on Tuesdays." In "No Speak English," Mamacita, who can only speak Spanish, is confined by language. On one level, these limits offer the safety of familiarity, but Esperanza, in recognizing that they are limits to freedom and individuality, also sees that they imprison. In making the comparison, Esperanza is able to challenge narrow perceptions and understandings. She is able to cross borders and move beyond the choices the women of her culture and neighborhood have made.[11]

Esperanza also uses the stories in her neighborhood to illustrate her ideals as she wavers between the worlds of childhood and adulthood. She experiences the enchantment of emerging sexuality, in "The Family of Little Feet," when she and her friends, Lucy and Rachel, put on a neighbor's castaway high heels. The girls experience a Cinderella moment when they look down at their high-heeled feet and discover their own long legs, their womanhood. When the girls practice walking in their heels, they are ogled and whistled at, recognizing a desire that frightens them and makes them wish to remain a bit longer in the world of childhood.[12]

Still Esperanza looks to her world for examples to define her sexuality and autonomy. She imagines herself with a boy named Sire, but she wants also to control the relationship. When she takes a job, an old man who befriends her makes her uncomfortable with a kiss on the lips. That frightens Esperanza because she can not stop it. When Esperanza's friend Sally leaves her alone and she is molested, Esperanza cries out against her isolation, her lack of power to stop the boys.[13]

Through these experiences, roles and expectations of adult women shift for Esperanza. She wants control, strength, and autonomy. While she might understand that the expectations for a grown woman in her neighborhood are to marry and raise a family, she does not know if this is what she wants. But she finds solace and strength in writing, and she will turn to that to empower her life.

Since the publication of *The House on Mango Street,* Cisneros's work has continued to portray the oppression of women, particularly the Chicana woman. But she admits now that she is older and more aware of the power of stories, she also wants to know more about the men she writes about. She must dispel ego to get inside a character's motivation and concentrate on doing this for community good. "Each book gets harder," Cisneros says, and sometimes she feels terror at facing the page; other times she despairs. But the payoff of getting a story into the world is worth the terror and despair. "That's what I feel literature is about. We can actually save lives, we can, through story, change the world and make it better."[14]

CHAPTER 4

Poetic Devices

While the language and poetic structure of
The House on Mango Street demonstrates choices of
simplicity and spare text, metaphors take on sig-
nificant meaning when images are repeated in the
vignettes that comprise the novel. For example,
Cisneros places women near windows to illustrate
the limits of their view against the backdrop of
community and the larger world.

Esperanza imagines her great-grandmother,
her namesake, who was forced to marry, sadly sitting at her window, watching her life pass by. The
neighbor Rafaela, locked inside her apartment

when her husband goes out, calls the girls to her window and lowers money down to have them purchase coconuts and papaya juice while she dreams of dancing. Minerva, the neighbor who also writes poetry, is trapped inside her house with two children she raises alone and a husband who comes and goes. When she finally sends her husband packing, he throws a rock through her window, shattering her small world. She opens the door to him once again only to have the scene repeated over and over. When Esperanza's friend Sally marries, she, too, is locked inside her home and her husband will not even let her look outside the window.[1]

The house Esperanza lives in has windows that reflect her fears that she is also living the trapped existence of these women. The top-floor windows are barred so that the women in her family will not fall out. The windows below that are "so small you'd think they were holding their breath."[2]

Trees also take on significance in Esperanza's world. She had hoped to find a lush backyard with a healthy tree to climb when she moved to Mango Street. Instead, there are four spindly elms that the city planted outside in front. The more she looks at them, the more they take on the significance of survival for Esperanza. In "Four Skinny Trees," the trees are personified to take on resilience, strength, and independence. Esperanza imagines that, as a group, the trees are able to communicate to one another. In communicating, they support one another and even work together to hold one another up. Esperanza believes the trees are telling her to persevere, and she becomes determined to be more like the trees.[3]

When Esperanza puts on her neighbor's high heels and discovers a taste of adulthood, it becomes obvious that shoes are a metaphor for childhood and adulthood. Brown school shoes depict Esperanza's self-conscious childishness in

"Chanclas." In this scene, Esperanza is forced to wear her old saddle shoes with a new dress because her mother did not buy her new shoes. When Esperanza goes to the dance, she is self-conscious and afraid to dance. Even after an uncle pulls her onto the dance floor and Esperanza dances, she remains embarrassed by the way her feet feel awkward, big and "heavy like plungers."[4]

Esperanza is conscious of other people's shoes, noticing and even desiring Sally's black suede shoes in the scene where she wants to befriend the more precocious Sally. Later on, when Sally leaves Esperanza to play kissing games with some boys in the neighborhood, Esperanza waits and notices her own feet look foreign. Finally, when Esperanza imagines having her own space or her own house, shoes neatly aligned with the bed symbolize her sense of belonging in her own house and living her own way.[5]

In many instances, Cisneros uses references to poetry or poetic phrases to portray the movements within the vignettes. The girls practice jump-rope chants, and we discover that Esperanza's sister, Nenny, who always goes back to the old rhymes, lacks the imagination of the older girls, who use poetry to imagine different lives. There are references to Minerva's and Rafaela's poetry, both references to the ways these young women dream and wish to live differently.[6]

It is no accident that some paragraphs within the vignettes contain rhyme and metaphor. "This is a postmodern form of fiction stitching together a series of lyrical pieces, 'lazy poems,' Cisneros calls them."[7]

It is with intention and drive that Esperanza compares herself to her surroundings. She tells this story in first person with the language she has mastered as though, as narrator, she is also the writer. By writing and telling her story, Esperanza has gained control of her past. "She has created a present in which she can be free and belong at the same time. Her freedom is the narrativity. Mango Street will always be a part of this woman, but she has taken the strength of trees into herself and has found the courage to be the house of her dreams, her own self-invention."[8]

CHAPTER 5

The Character of Esperanza Cordero

The House on Mango Street is a personal and sensory narrative that invites readers in to experience the angst of Esperanza and the other female characters in the novel. While Esperanza develops as a woman, she also develops a unique and strong voice, one that not only speaks for herself but also offers hope to other women caught in the clash of cultures.[1]

Esperanza's story, told in the first person narrative through her eyes, is about the changes that occur when Esperanza is twelve, the year she emerges from childhood into adulthood. As she emerges from childhood through her watching, listening,

Sandra Cisneros as a freshman in high school, about the same age as Esperanza Cordero, the main character in the novel. Although the fictional character is not meant to be a mirror image of the author, Esperanza goes through the same emotions and struggles Cisneros did growing up.

and dreaming, Esperanza paints her family's history and their lives. It is a traditional Mexican–American family surviving in a Chicago barrio.[2]

While exploring her own emerging sexuality and adulthood, Esperanza reflects on what it means to be a woman by analyzing the evolving roles of women and the cultural roles they each bring from various Chicano backgrounds. She compares contemporary relationships to those of the older women in the neighborhood and to those of her ancestors. Esperanza looks at the unequal or disparate roles between boys and girls in her community and sees that to follow these established traditions, she will limit her own possibilities. She sees her peers' acceptance of their parents' traditions as the decision of young women to choose the less desirable house of her neighborhood. These houses controlled by the men come to symbolize traditional female roles. Esperanza bemoans her friends' choices, noticing that Marin conforms to tradition, working to look beautiful, hoping that men will find her attractive so that someone will marry her and take her to a "big house" far away.[3]

But the patriarchal world of her cultural traditions proves to be a world suffused with abuse, both physical and sexual. Critics define this as a world that reinforces the idea that a woman is an object to be owned and controlled, rarely perceived as a full human being. Esperanza stands out as distanced from her friends Sally and Alicia who fear their fathers because she does not have to fear her own. She scorns the idea that a house must enclose and imprison each girl or woman. She recognizes the inferior life that many of the women around her must lead if they follow tradition. This is not the choice that Esperanza will make. With unfolding knowledge of her choices, Esperanza also emerges as a character who can maneuver between the world of two languages. This gives her freedom that others do not have. This signals her comfort with both worlds, her ability to interact with a world outside of her culture. This comfort allows women like Esperanza to speak out in "a rush of words whose flow will not be stemmed."[4]

CHAPTER 6

The Corderos' World—Culture, Class, and Stereotypes

Esperanza's family is constrained by cultural traditions and poverty. Cisneros describes the Mexican culture that is Esperanza's as a matriarchal culture that is also a macho society. Esperanza recognizes that men control the world but women, by participating, control the family. The model of love that Cisneros portrays through Esperanza's eyes is one in which true love is not always between two lovers. It can be mothers and sons, fathers and daughters, grandmothers and granddaughters, sisters. True love is family.[1]

When Esperanza's parents promise that the family will live in a house that can be a home, Esperanza discovers the disappointment of this shabby house on Mango Street. The discovery sets Esperanza on the journey to find out who she is. She wants to find the house that stands in as a metaphor for her identity. She expresses disappointment and mourns the house of her dreams. Her parents assure her that, while this is the first house that they own, this is only temporary. Esperanza "will not give up her dream of the promised house and will pursue it."[2]

Still, she mourns the ragged house, and this mourning sets her apart from her family. Soon she recognizes other differences from her family. For instance, in "Hairs," she describes physical differences in the way each family member's hair has different textures, from curly to slippery. Her mother's hair smells like bread.[3] Differences in the worlds between boys and girls are also explored. Her brothers Carlos and Kiki are each others' best friends, but not best friends with Esperanza or her sister, Nenny.[4]

While she learns from the men in her neighborhood about the way machismo can keep a woman in her place, she learns from her father that the world contains some good men. Her father represents fathers who work hard and long to support their families, rising from their beds before dawn. She learns that these men, men like her father, are not afraid to show emotion. After telling Esperanza that her *abuelito,* or grandfather, has died, her father "crumbles like a coat and cries." She holds him in her arms and offers what comfort she can.[5]

Esperanza's most important lessons are those she receives through the love and examples of her mother who gave up her education out of shame over her poverty.[6]

Esperanza wants more from her life than her parents dream for her. She openly revolts after her mother tells her that she will settle down one day. Instead she proclaims, "I have decided not to grow up tame like the others who lay their necks on the threshold waiting for the ball and chain."[7]

In defying tradition, she is determining her own independence, admitting that she has discovered the individual within. In beginning what she refers to as her own quiet war, "Esperanza refuses to join the ranks of Mexican-American women who serve men."[8]

It is small wonder that, because of the important journey to independence and autonomy that Esperanza takes, *The House on Mango Street* has sold over two million copies. It has become a shared novel in a number of cities as part of recent library efforts to encourage reading and discussion about major works in communities throughout the United States.

CHAPTER 7

Other Works

Cisneros's first book was a small collection of poems, entitled *Bad Boys*. This chapbook was published in 1980 by Mango Press, a Latino press located in San Jose, California. For two years before this, Cisneros had worked teaching high-school dropouts while writing *The House on Mango Street* in the evening at her kitchen table. Only after she received a National Endowment of the Arts grant was she able to take some time to finish the book.

The House on Mango Street, published by Arte Público Press in Houston,[1] surprised critics and readers alike when, through word of mouth, it became a popular novel for adults and young adults. Before long, it drew the attention of a major publisher, who republished the work.

Despite her success, the financial stability necessary to make a living as a writer eluded Cisneros at first. She worked as a teacher and a college recruiter before receiving a fellowship and moving to Texas to complete a book of poetry. Themes that revolved around Mexican and Mexican-American women who find the strength to rise about the poverty of their surroundings found their way into *My Wicked Wicked Ways*, published in 1987.[2] This collection celebrated those bad girls who find their hearts also filled with virtue.[3] Still, she described the beginning of 1987 as the worst year of her life:

> I was alienated; I was in a new city, I did not
> know anyone; I was in a new job with just a lot of
> pressure to succeed, and I put a lot of demands
> on myself. . . . I was in a great place of depres-
> sion because I felt that I couldn't make a living

from my writing. I wasn't very good, I thought,

as a professor because of my first semester. I was

really hard on myself. I felt like a failure. I

didn't want to borrow money again to leave

because I had to borrow money to get there. . . .

I felt trapped.[4]

But 1987 improved greatly, in fact becoming the best year of her life. Agent Susan Bergholz took Cisneros on as a client and Random House, recognizing the value of Latina literature in a climate when schools were seeking quality multicultural literature, agreed to publish her work. Cisneros had begun a novel, but that was difficult and so she also began working on short stories. One in particular kept coming back to her. It was a story based upon a young mulatto woman that Cisneros had seen on a family trip to Acapulco. That mulatto woman, whose name was Candelaria and who had the most beautiful caramel-colored skin, became the central character of her second novel. "I saw her a couple of seconds in my life, and I wondered all these years why she stayed with me."[5]

Cisneros went back to the novel but nothing came easily. During that time, Cisneros had moved to California to teach at California State University in Chico, California. A second National Endowment of the Arts grant came through and helped her to complete her second novel, which took almost a decade to produce. It was called *Caramelo*. "There were times during the process of writing this book that I really was lost. In the fifth year and sixth year I was in deep despair," Cisneros recalls about her process. "I was very blocked and frightened by the deadline and the enormity of what I had created. I was just trying to tell a simple tale and it had just gotten all out of hand."[6]

While the novel grew from a simple story of a father and daughter into a massive accounting of ancestry and Mexican-American crossings, Cisneros's poetry continued to be published. *My*

Wicked Wicked Ways immersed readers in Chicano life. The first half of the collection even describes Cisneros's own home in San Antonio. The second half of this poetry collection leaves the barrio behind, and the author's world becomes more cosmopolitan but more personal, too. In this collection, Cisneros reflects on the ways men and women treat one another. Some of it is her own personal story of how she treats men and they treat her.

Called "not only a gifted writer, but an absolutely essential one" by the *New York Times Book Review,* Cisneros established herself as an author of "electrifying talent" with this collection of poetry. The lines of verses reflect comedy and sadness through pure and simple language. When comparing the power of language in her poetry to the language of her short stories, critics declared her poetry and stories should be praised for their precision and musicality of language.[7]

Of the variety in her writing, Cisneros says, "Sometimes you have to write a little note; sometimes you have to write a letter." The new novel, which was becoming a novel of epic proportions, must have loomed large in her mind when she added, "Sometimes you need a hammer; sometimes you need a screw."[8]

In 1994, *Loose Woman,* a collection of poetry told in three parts, was released. The three parts have been described as a spirited collection that addresses the heart. The collection introduces readers to yet another "powerful, fiercely independent woman of Mexican heritage, though this time innocence has long been lost. For her the worlds of language and life are one and the same." The narrator laments, "'Lorenzo, I forget what's real. / I mix up the details of what happened / with what I witnessed inside my / universe.'" *Publishers Weekly* described the poems as "short-lined, chantlike, biting."[9]

Reviewer Barbara Hoffert wrote of the collection in the *Library Journal,* "The poems that result are brilliant and shimmering and sharp-tongued and just occasionally a little too similar. Highly recommended where good poetry is read and essential for all Hispanic collections."[10]

The language of the poems is seductive and lively. "You bring out the Mexican in me. / The hunkered thick dark spiral. / The core of a heart howl. / The bitter bile. . . ."[11]

While Cisneros is addressing a lover, she could well be addressing the act of writing itself, along with the passion she associates with her Mexican roots.[12] The *Boston Globe* review called the collection "a candid, sexy and wonderfully mood-strewn collection of poetry that celebrates the female aspects of love, from the reflective to the overtly erotic. Poignant, sexy . . . lyrical, passionate . . . cool and delicate . . . hot as a chili pepper."[13]

Through these poems, Cisneros speaks for and calls for women who love themselves enough to love men who are brave enough to love them back. The language is refreshing in its simplicity; "[the] voice draws from her native Spanish, from bedroom banter, and occasionally from the gutter. Yet it is always poetic, founded upon vivid imagery, subtle rhythm and musical sounds."[14]

Loose Woman challenges the gender stereotypes of the passive and pure Mexican woman. This is no surprise, when readers consider that Cisneros challenges herself, her culture, and the traditions within her own community, often speaking out for the rights of women and immigrants and working to improve education for both.

Sometimes challenges even seem to knock at her front door. After Sandra Cisneros purchased a house in a historic district in San Antonio and painted it purple, city commissioners took issue with the color. Cisneros, herself, took issue with the

Sandra Cisneros's controversial purple house in San Antonio, Texas. This photograph was taken after the paint had some time to fade into a "more acceptable" color.

fact that commissioners failed to recognize the history of her culture within the district. She argued that the bright purple paint "Mexicanized" the 1903 metal-roofed Victorian in San Antonio's historic King William district. Cisneros argued, "The issue is bigger than my house. The issue is about historical inclusion. . . . Purple is historic to us. It only goes back a thousand years or so to the pyramids. It is present in the Nahua codices, book of the Aztecs, as is turquoise, the color I used for my house trim; the former color signifying royalty, the latter, water and rain."[15]

The controversy received national media attention. But the debate died down two years later when the paint had faded to a pale blue, which was deemed acceptable.[16]

Shortly before the paint issue was resolved, one of Cisneros's vignettes, "Hairs," was produced as a children's picture book titled *Hairs/Pelitos*. "Everybody in our family has different hair" / "Todos en nuestra familia tenemos pelo diferente," begins this bilingual book taken from a vignette in Cisneros's *The House on Mango Street*. This illustrated picture book shows portraits of the diversity among us. Awarded *Parenting Magazine's* Best Children's Book of the Year and published in 1994, this book was described as an "an affectionate picture of familial love and a cozy bedtime book."[17]

Despite these publications, Cisneros's financial situation remained tenuous. She continued to struggle to live on the proceeds from her writing, fearing that to take on more teaching would interfere with looming writing deadlines. Her second novel was not finished. "It's difficult for me to have a large story, a very large story—a novel is a large story. I'm used to writing and doing these little miniature paintings. Now I've got this huge canvas, and it's hard for me to look at it as a whole," she explains.[18] She returned again to a form that came more readily—her short stories. *Woman Hollering Creek* was the result.

This collection relied upon characters that portray life on both sides of the Mexican border. The tales of the women's lives in these stories capture moments of discovery. Some are wise and many are intimate. The *Library Journal* called Cisneros "a writer of vivid imagination, with a very acute sense of mysticism and a witty poetic style." The review called the collection "a key work from a major Hispanic American writer; recommended for public libraries." The review said of the author, "Cisneros not only entertains but leaves a lasting impression." Stories include a tale of a little girl revealing secrets as children do and a witch who flies at dawn over a small town.[19]

In this collection, Cisneros explores voice. The stories portray buoyant, strong, funny, and sad women. The brief vignettes of the opening piece, "My Lucy Friend Who Smells Like Corn," have been referred to as "tiles in a mosaic." Taken together, the stories offer a picture of lives on the Texas-Mexico border where family ties are strong and multi-generational. Families include aunts, uncles, cousins, and grandparents. Many of the stories focus on the romantic dreams of young girls who long to escape small towns only to discover things are much the same on the other side of the border.

Cisneros begins her novels with self-conscious but spontaneous young girls, but she often watches them turn to young women as the writing progresses. Her characters share "uneasy awareness that their self-worth depends on a loyalty to Mexico strained, all the same, by the realities of their lives up North." The restless bad girl of "Never Marry a Mexican" studies the conflict of a young Mexican-American woman, unable to speak Spanish, who feels foolish as "a Mexican girl who couldn't even speak Spanish," and also feels contempt for her white lover and his wife. The feminist stories reflect important border issues such as cultural imperialism.[20]

No matter what Cisneros is writing, she always challenges herself to do something she has not done before. "I know when I was writing *Woman Hollering Creek,* each story was a literary hurdle. So, for example, I did a monologue; well, then in the next piece I would try not to do the same thing over again. I'd say, okay, I already did that, so how can I make this different? I would try to set up some situation where I could do something new, and it was usually influenced by whom I was reading at the time."[21]

Even while Cisneros worked on the short stories, her novel about the relationship between a girl and her father preoccupied her. She returned to it. While writing *Caramelo,* Cisneros's father died of cancer. This father and daughter had survived many conflicts including Cisneros's desire to avoid marriage, to live on her own, and to live as a writer. He saw her take her career seriously, to the point of not marrying and quitting jobs. He saw her making sacrifices that women make for husbands. "I always called the writing my husband," Cisneros says. "I also call 'him' the wife-beater. The writing has been that, abusive and supportive and loving and also a very difficult marriage, and my father just couldn't understand why I just couldn't settle down with someone who'd take care of me, and have kids."[22] Despite their conflicts, Cisneros loved her father dearly. "This book was for my father," she says. "I created this story to fill in gaps so that I could understand my father and to write his history."[23]

In 2002, *Caramelo* was unveiled. Cisneros's original intent had been to write a simple story of a father and his daughter. But it became an epic novel of more than six hundred pages that also captures the history of Mexican migration and border crossings. The story of a father and his daughter's lives grew to encompass many generations of a Mexican-American family. The novel is told with humor, passion, and poignancy. Maria Newman, a reviewer, says, "In *Caramelo* she [Cisneros] empties her notebook and her heart on issues that she has been musing on all of her life: love, her father, the relationship between fathers and daughters, the relationship of a Mexican man with his wife and mother, and a spider's web of memory and remembrance and the music that accompanied them."[24]

The novel's plot centers on the way culture is passed down from one generation to another by the women in this family. It tells the tale of Lala Reyes's grandmother, descended from a family of renowned *rebozo,* or shawl, makers. The striped caramelo rebozo is the most beautiful of all. This shawl makes its way, like the family history it has come to represent, into Lala's possession. *Caramelo* is also the story of this granddaughter's relationship with her grandmother and their connection through Lala's father. Reminiscent of stories Cisneros has told of her own family's travels to Mexico, the novel opens with the Reyes family's annual car trip in a caravan overflowing with children, from Chicago to "the other side," which is Mexico City. Each year in Mexico City, Lala hears her family's stories and learns to separate the truth from the "healthy lies" that have traveled down the generations. The novel encompasses scenes of Mexico City, the music-filled streets of Chicago during the Roaring Twenties, and Lala's difficult adolescence in San Antonio, Texas.[25]

In a starred review for *Booklist,* critic Keir Graff wrote of the novel, "Cisneros combines a real respect for history with a playful sense of how lies often tell the greatest truths—the characters, narrator, and author all play fast and loose with the facts. But Lala learns the ability to write your own history also means you must take special care in choosing your fate. The author's gorgeous prose, on-a-dime turns of phrase, and sumptuous scene-setting make this an unforgettable read."[26]

Subtle use of language creates the bicultural world in *Caramelo.* With imagery that surprises, stories surface within stories, creating the unreality of Latin-American magical realism. "Unexpected twists bring to mind García Márquez, Juan Rulfo and the Isabel Allende of *House of the Spirits*," writes reviewer Margaret Randall. "But Cisneros has moved beyond those authors and their novels. She weaves a new fabric of Spanish, English and Spanglish, and in so doing reflects the particular symbiosis of the Mexican-American and American-Mexican cultures that blossomed in this part of the world as the twentieth century unfolded."[27]

Cisneros faces issues of privilege in these stories. "Race, the privilege bestowed by lighter skin, gender, sexuality, class and the love-hate relationship that characterizes Mexicans and US Americans are handled with a delicate touch but the most nuanced complexity," says Randall.[28]

One way Cisneros accomplishes the nuanced complexity of these relationships is by translating some Spanish terms or phrases into "absolutely literal English." The meaning beneath the meaning comes through with such clarity, it shakes readers into awareness.[29]

"This is not a family memoir," comments Cisneros. "A lot of people are going to take it as that. They always take my writing as factual. It's fact-based but I just use it as a springboard."[30]

The novel was considered by many to demonstrate the maturity and growth of the poet who penned *The House on Mango Street.* "When I wrote House, I was a very inexperienced fiction writer because I was trained as a poet. . . . With this book I wanted to expand and grow and do something that I hadn't done before and handle all the people that I knew growing up, all the cousins and uncles, the family that I could recall that I hadn't written about in House because that was not my focus."[31]

In writing about the relationships between grandmothers and their granddaughters, Cisneros sought to demythologize the grandmother. She hopes this will allow contemporary women freedom to live their lives without feeling as though they must become a tribute to their grandmothers. In doing so, she criticized her elders, often a taboo among Chicano writers. "We are our ancestors, including the ones we don't like. . . . [W]e fit into each other, like these nesting cups. Once I knew that as an author, then I could start being generous with her [the grandmother] as a character. She's still awful, but I have more empathy, and I could understand her. Therefore, the book took me to a real spiritual place and moved me from siding with my mother. Not necessarily that I side with my grandmother, but I'm kind of above both of them, and I can see them clearly."[32]

This novel also captures the heartbreak many immigrants suffer when they cross borders. Its success earned Cisneros the unexpected role of spokesperson for immigration issues at a time when anti-immigrant sentiments had grown in the United States. The sudden celebrity, in turn, makes it more difficult for Cisneros to focus on her writing. She works to balance the two through meditation practices developed through her Buddhist faith, coupled with her Latino spiritual beliefs. From her Catholic upbringing, the writer continues to have

Author Sandra Cisneros sports a tattoo of the Virgin of Guadalupe sitting in a meditative position, depicting her Buddhist and Catholic spiritual beliefs. The Virgin of Guadalupe has been a very important religious and cultural image to the Mexican people since the sixteenth century.

strong loyalty to the Virgin of Guadalupe, so she playfully refers to herself as a "Buddhalupist."[33]

In 2004, Vintage Books included Cisneros on the publisher's list of great modern writers with the publication of *Vintage Cisneros*. This collection features an excerpt from Cisneros's best seller *The House on Mango Street*. Also included are a chapter from the novel *Caramelo*; poems from *My Wicked Wicked Ways* and *Loose Woman*; and seven stories from her award-winning collection *Woman Hollering Creek*.

Cisneros's current writing projects include poetry, short stories, and another novel. She is also at work on a book about writing called *Writing in My Pajamas*. Illustrating her own teaching methods, the book focuses on the way a writer thinks about formal and informal language. She explains that she tells her students to get rid of formal language and write as though they are talking to someone they are so comfortable with, they would not even have to be dressed.[34]

CHAPTER 8

The Importance of This Work

Only four years after it first hit bookstores, *The House on Mango Street* had won the prestigious Before Columbus Foundation's American Book Award and a fourth edition had been printed. Since then, it has been translated into a number of languages and remains a steady best seller.[1]

As a city-wide reading program choice, theme-related entertainment and events, including author visits, have become part of Cisneros's life. The cities of Miami, Seattle, and Milwaukee have chosen *The House on Mango Street* as their city-wide title. She tells audiences that, although she never intended to write a coming-of-age classic, she knew even while writing *The House on Mango Street* that it would transcend generations. She asks, "Have you ever had those moments of clairvoyance? I felt it in my heart, so I knew it was true." Cisneros says she deliberately wrote *Mango Street* so that a diverse group of readers could enjoy it, from high-school students, to mothers, to taxi drivers. "I tried to write it in a way that was all inclusive," she explains. "I tried to write in simple language, so that all ages could read it." While *The House on Mango Street* has become a popular choice for city-wide reading programs, she reminds readers that it was anything but an overnight success.[2]

Inclusion in programs like this does not necessarily amaze Cisneros. Instead, it is the many letters she has received over the years. Readers, many of them college students who first read *Mango Street* in middle school, have written Cisneros, telling her the book helped them take control of their own lives. She says, "When I get those types of testimonials, that just gives me *escalofrios*, you know, shivers."[3]

The House on Mango Street made Cisneros one of the most well read of Latino authors, selling more than two million copies by 2002. It is often assigned as reading for high school and college courses and, over the years, it has received recognition and awards. Because the novel made Cisneros a voice for issues of identity and immigration, in July 1995, she received the prestigious MacArthur Fellowship.[4] The fellowship is a five-year grant to artists "who show exceptional creativity in their work and the prospect for still more in the future." The fellowship allows recipients the flexibility to pursue their creative activities. This award made it possible for Cisneros finally to rely on her writing to live.[5]

In 2002, when the city of Miami made *The House on Mango Street* the selected reading for their

One Book, One Community program, newspapers described the impact of the book in schools: "*The House on Mango Street* became a hit among teachers because it was 'a work of art' that was not very long and whose subject and language were appropriate for teenagers in a classroom." According to one such teacher, Carl Jago, the book came at the right time, when many teachers were desperately looking for a Latino writer to bring into classrooms.[6]

Many teachers agree that Latina fiction, and *The House on Mango Street,* in particular, can encourage students to develop their own adolescent voices. Leslie Averback, who chairs her middle-school's English department in Hoboken, New Jersey, says that the classroom has become a place to promote adolescents' social, emotional, and intellectual development. In doing so, teachers encourage their students to discover "that literature is a playing ground for the discovery of what it means to be human." Using strong literature about exploring self-identity can help students to "experiment with different identities and ideas." Averback believes that, if teachers encourage students to immerse themselves in the world created by characters such as Esperanza Cordoza, they can encourage their students "to become open to the thoughts, emotions, conflicts and resolutions of those characters, and to learn more about themselves and their potential for growth from the experience." Averback explains it is especially important for works such as *The House on Mango Street* to be brought into classrooms because teens today experience the unfamiliar faster than they can process their experiences.[7]

A female perspective is especially important in a culture that encourages girls to exchange strong voices for the more reserved, appeasing voices that have historically been encouraged. Teen girls, in particular, can become isolated, confused, and alienated while they struggle with identity. Many can relate to Esperanza's low self-esteem. *The House on Mango Street* offers them an alternative.[8] Through Esperanza, readers gain knowledge of a world in which females struggle to survive poverty and abuse. But, even if this world is new to them, they discover the power of the journey to find out who they want to become as adults.[9]

The novel is also frequently used in bilingual classrooms with students for whom English is a second language. Because the vignettes are written in simple, straightforward language, the novel has served to help these students discover the beauty and power of sensory language. Through Esperanza's story, they learn that English can be effective in evoking emotion while it explores important issues such as race, gender, ethnicity, and social class. *The House on Mango Street* opens the way for teens to hear words for their beauty, to visualize the images they convey, and it gives teens new to English the opportunity to recreate images through their own creative process.[10]

Cisneros believes this novel, like all of her work, helps to break down stereotypes. While her characters live in a world that can be very different from the United States that many have assimilated into, her characters "live, love and laugh in the flowing cadences of the Spanish language." "I'm the mouse who puts a thorn in the lion's paw," Cisneros says when contemplating the way her stories and poetry jar readers beyond their assumptions.[11]

The House on Mango Street changes thinking and understanding of cultures. It can also bridge the gap between cultures. While teaching in an upper middle-class private school, one teacher tells the story of bringing the novel into her classroom to help her wealthy students understand elements of privilege set against issues of culture and class. Teacher Kathleen Ryan asserts that students make personal connections when the book they read allows them to experience someone else's life. This book was an important step in helping students to experience the way race, class, and gender might arise in a world where cultures clash or blend. "Like Esperanza my students, too, were figuring out who they wanted to be," says Ryan. "But because Esperanza faces class and cultural challenges with which most of my students were unfamiliar, as we read Esperanza's story, my students began to investigate these issues."[12]

Most readers recognize that ethnicity is a presence in Cisneros's work and personal life. This focus actually came out of her own experience as a graduate student at the Iowa Writers Workshop in 1978, when Cisneros realized her voice as a writer came from her Mexican-American experience. Her differences from the other students became her unique voice and subject. In writing about her culture and class, she transformed the reality of economic and ethnic marginalization into a positive identity. "By the beginning of her second year at Iowa, her poems about the neighborhoods she lived in as a youth were well received in class." They also offer a realistic portrait of the Latino barrio. Her stories tell the reality of poor neighborhoods that lose their charm after dark or when the garbage is not picked up or when people become drunk and violent. Her work is also unique because it does not come from a male perspective. "I was writing about it in the most real sense that I knew, as a [woman] walking those neighborhoods. . . . I saw it a lot differently than all those 'chingones' that are writing all those [phony] pieces about their barrios," she said.[13]

Cisneros admits that when she was younger she was unaware of the possible effect of her work. She says, "I think that because all those issues are inside me already, that if I just write from that very deep place and if I take the writing far enough, all of those issues will come out anyway without me getting on a soapbox. The world becomes political just by me writing from my passions."[14]

The House on Mango Street reflects a passionate understanding of what it means to seek freedom outside the society of the neighborhood, beyond feminine limitations that have been set by tradition, class, and home life. It also speaks to the importance of putting a hand out to help raise others up, which occurs when Esperanza promises to return to Mango Street and help those who have not found their way out of the limitations set on them.

In choosing the novel as a community-wide read, communities celebrate the value of the importance that is Esperanza. It is a value that is not lost on Cisneros. "I value very much, if not most, my right to speak without being thrown in jail or killed—this is my American inheritance. Of my Mexican inheritance, I'd say it's the spirituality, the generosity, the cariño [love], the resilience."[15]

The House on Mango Street has brought tremendous success to Cisneros who received a number of grants, fellowships, and awards for this and other works. But her father was never really able to understand her success, she says. She explained, "If your parents are from another culture, they know you've received a lot of money, but they don't know what the NEA grant is." He was with the author once when she had to deposit an early [MacArthur] grant check, one of many that Cisneros received over the five years that the grant was providing for her livelihood. He took a picture, which she still has, of herself holding the check for $35,000.[16]

Cisneros says her father was also with her the day she bought her car with part of her advance for *Woman Hollering Creek*. "That was another moment," says the author. "He looked at my check and said,

THE REALITY OF LABELS

When Sandra Cisneros saw a sign advertising Valenzuela's Latino Bookstore in San Antonio, Texas, she was sure she had discovered a treasure. The independent bookseller's Latina name appealed directly to her as a Latina writer.

The sign proved to be more than she had hoped for, though. When Cisneros entered the store, a clerk used a word to describe the Latina/o section of books that offended Cisneros. "She used the word Hispanic," Cisneros says. "I wanted to ask her, 'Why are you using that word?'

"People who use that word don't know why they're using it," says Cisneros. "To me, it's like a slave name. I'm a Latina."[19]

That word illustrates a debate over how Spanish-speaking people might identify themselves as a group. Are they Hispanics or Latinos?

Although many believe the two terms can be interchanged, experts say their meanings can be traced "to the original bloodlines of Spanish speakers to different populations in opposite parts of the world."[20]

Hispanics are from the Iberian Peninsula (Spain and Portugal). Latinos and Latinas descend from the indigenous peoples of Mexico, Central America, South America, and the Caribbean, regions Spain conquered long ago.

According to these experts "Latino-Hispanic is an ethnic category that includes people of any race. They are white . . . and black. . . . They can also be Indian and Asian. Many are mixtures of several races."[21]

As a poet, Cisneros is especially sensitive to the power a single word can wield. She says, "It's not a word, it's a way of looking at the world. It's a way of looking at meaning."[22]

The term Hispanic was promoted by the Nixon administration in 1970 when it was added to the census questionnaire as a race. By 1980, it had become an official government term, appearing on census forms and employment, general assistance, and school enrollment applications.

Some Mexican-American activists prefer using a term that includes the indigenous Indians who were their ancestors.[23]

'Ah, the years I would have had to work to earn this amount.'"[17]

Two things finally made him understand that Cisneros is indeed a professional writer. "One was the MacArthur, not because he understood what the MacArthur was, but because he understood the amount ($255,000). The other thing was that he saw Carlos Fuentes on Spanish-language TV and Carlos Fuentes mentioned my name as one of the writers he admired. That my father understood."[18]

Cisneros's stories and outspoken courage add up to the passion that has helped her develop a revolutionary sense of justice. She has refused to allow her work to be included in anthologies that use the term *Hispanic,* a word coined by the federal government to identify Spanish-speaking people for a 1970 U.S. census. She also refused to be photographed for a Gap ad because she did not believe the clothing company demonstrated a strong commitment to Latino communities.

She has become an outspoken advocate for Latino writers, saying, "I tell students, you really should not be glad that I'm the only Latina that's getting published. You should be ashamed. Why am I the only one? That's a question that we have to ask." She also encourages better education for Latinos. "I don't want young people in the barrios to see me as a kind of an example of pull your selves up by the bootstraps. I really want them to question the educational system and the whole system that is created to keep them from becoming what I became." She labels herself a translator, an amphibian, a traveler in two worlds, explaining, "I have the power to make people think in a different way. It's a different way of defining power, and it is something that I don't want to abuse or lose. I want to help my community."[24]

When Cisneros is teaching, her advice to young writers is not about publishing or money. It is about writing from the heart, writing because you feel you must. "If I'm talking to really young women," says the author, "I tell them to get an education and get a library card. I tell them to become economically independent because you have to presume you'll never make any money from your writing—and making money isn't a measure of the worth of your writing." Cisneros sees many young writers who desperately want to get published. "I always tell young writers to be in a hurry to become a good writer. The publishing will take care of itself."[25]

CHAPTER 9

Best-Seller Lists and Awards

Sandra Cisneros's work broke new ground when she became one of the first Latina writers to be read in college and high-school classrooms. Since then, she has won numerous awards. Not only has *The House on Mango Street* been selected for the many One-City/One-Read programs, but *Caramelo* has been included in these projects in communities including Los Angeles, Miami, Fort Worth, El Paso, and Milwaukee.

Woman Hollering Creek and Other Stories was awarded the PEN Center West Award for Best Fiction of 1991, the Quality Paperback Book Club New

Sandra Cisneros lectures at Cornell University on September 13, 2007, as part of the Creative Writing Reading series, inspiring the next generation of authors.

Voices Award, the Anisfield-Wolf Book Award, the Lannan Foundation Literary Award; it was selected as a noteworthy book of the year by *The New York Times* and *The American Library Journal*, and nominated Best Book of Fiction for 1991 by the *Los Angeles Times*. *Loose Woman* won the Mountains & Plains Booksellers' Award.

In 1995, Cisneros was awarded the prestigious MacArthur Foundation Fellowship, and subsequently organized the Latino MacArthur Fellows—Los MacArturos—into a reunion that focuses on community outreach. In 2003, she was awarded the Texas Medal of the Arts.

She has received many other honors, including an honorary Doctor of Humane Letters from Loyola University, Chicago, 2002; an honorary Doctor of Letters from the State University of New York at Purchase, 1993; two National Endowment of the Arts Fellowships for fiction and poetry, 1988, 1982; the Roberta Holloway Lectureship at the University of California, Berkeley, 1988; the Chicano Short Story Award from the University of Arizona, 1986; the Texas Institute of Letters Dobie Paisano Fellowship, 1985; and an Illinois Artists Grant, 1984.

Caramelo was selected as notable book of the year by several newspapers, including *The New York Times*, the *Los Angeles Times*, the *San Francisco Chronicle*, the *Chicago Tribune*, and *The Seattle Times*. In 2005,

Caramelo was awarded the Premio Napoli and was short listed for the Dublin International IMPAC Award. It was also nominated for the Orange Prize in England.

The author's books have been translated into more than a dozen languages, including Spanish, Galician, French, German, Dutch, Italian, Norwegian, Japanese, Chinese, Turkish, and, most recently, into Greek, Thai, and Serbo-Croatian.

Cisneros is the president and founder of the Macondo Foundation, an association of socially engaged writers working to advance creativity, foster generosity, and honor communities; and the Alfredo Cisneros Del Moral Foundation, a grant-giving institution serving Texas writers.[1]

Out of the love and respect she has for her parents who might not always have understood her need for a space of her own, and in memory of their support and encouragement for her writing, Cisneros created a foundation and scholarships for aspiring writers. After his death, the Alfredo Cisneros Del Moral Foundation was created in 2000 to honor the memory of Cisneros's father who earned his living as an upholsterer. "My father lived his life as an example of generosity and honest labor," Cisneros has written. "Even as he warned us to save our centavitos, he was always giving away his own. A meticulous craftsman, he would sooner rip the seams of a cushion apart and do it over than put his name on an item that wasn't up to his high standards. I especially wanted to honor his memory with an award showcasing writers who are equally proud of their own craft."[2]

According to the foundation's Web site, since it originated in 2007, the Alfredo Cisneros Del Moral Foundation has awarded more than $75,500 to writers born in Texas, writing about Texas, or living in Texas. "The Alfredo Cisneros Del Moral Foundation invites a panel of nominators to recommend writers from across writing disciplines who exhibit both exceptional talent and profound commitment to their chosen form of artistic expression."[3]

Sandra Cisneros has written of the importance of this award: "In my own experience, grants not only allowed me time to write, but, more importantly, confirmed I was indeed a writer at precarious moments when my own faith in my art wobbled." She hopes this award will strengthen the resolve of the award winners and further them in their own careers.[4]

When Cisneros's mother, Elvira "Vera" Cisneros, passed away in Chicago on November 1, 2007, at seventy-eight years old, Cisneros honored her with an article on her Web site. She wrote:

> While single and laboring in factories, Vera dreamed of a creative life. Her love of the Chicago Public Library, museums, and public concerts was instilled to all her children who

were able to rise from humble roots to become a doctor, an artist, an author, a musician, a geologist, and business owners. She channeled her own artistry into her garden. Extraordinarily intelligent, she was a self-made woman whose political insights could challenge and terrify any alderman or preacher. She never finished the ninth grade but favorite mentors were Noam Chomsky and Studs Terkel.[5]

In her mother's name, Cisneros created the Elvira Cordero Cisneros Scholarship Fund, for beneficiaries of the Macondo Foundation, the foundation she originated to help struggling writers.[6]

Cisneros's novels, short stories, and poetry have been anthologized and reprinted internationally. During 2009, she planned a national tour to celebrate the twenty-fifth anniversary of *The House on Mango Street*. She also continues to write. These days, she writes from her home in San

IN MACONDO LIBRE WHERE
WRITERS FIGHT TO WRITE

During a three-day period from July 30 through August 1, 2008, Cisneros hosted a Lucha Libre, a series of readings and music borrowed from the tradition of Mexican wrestling. The fund-raiser for the Macondo Foundation was publicized as an opportunity to watch renowned writers in the throes of "wrestling for truth and justice . . . where good conquers evil, our writers fight for political and social issues." A lucha poetry slam included performances by the poet Ai; poet, writer, and NPR commentator Andrei Codrescu; Sandra Cisneros, and musical performances by the father/son team George/Aaron Prado, the Krayolas, and other special guests. All proceeds from the event benefited Our Lady of the Lake University and the Macondo Foundation.[7]

Discussing the founding of the foundation in a press release, Cisneros said that it began as a workshop around her kitchen table in 1998. In less than nine years, the workshop grew from fifteen participants to more than one hundred twenty participants. The foundation also sponsors writers in a writer-in-residency program and continues to grow in its outreach to writers. Cisneros described the group "as an association of socially-engaged writers united to advance creativity, foster generosity, and honor community." She explained, "The Macondo Foundation attracts generous and compassionate writers who view their work and talents as part of a larger task of community-building and non-violent social change."[8]

Antonio in the company of many creatures including six dogs (Beto, Dante, Lolita, Chamaco, Valentina P-nut Butter, and Barney Fife), four cats (Gato Perón, Pánfilo, Apolonia, and Lulu), and a parrot named Agustina. As part of the biography she wrote for *The House on Mango Street,* Cisneros described herself: "I am nobody's mother, nobody's wife, am happily single and live in San Antonio, Texas, with the love of my life."[9]

She is currently at work on several projects, including a book about teaching writing with the working title *Writing in Your Pajamas,* and a collection of fiction titled *Infinito.*[10]

CHRONOLOGY

1954   Sandra Cisneros is born in Chicago, Illinois, to Alfredo and Elvira "Vera" Cisneros on December 20.

1976   Cisneros graduates from Loyola University in Chicago, Illinois, with a bachelor's degree in English.

1977   Cisneros's first publication, "To Startle Yourself: A Translation of Dario Ruiz Gomez's Work," is published in the *Denver Quarterly*.

1978   Cisneros graduates from the Iowa Writers Workshop with a master of fine arts in writing; her first poem, "Mexican Hat Dance," is published in *Nuestro* magazine.

1980   Cisneros's first book, a small collection of poems entitled *Bad Boys*, is published by Mango Press.

1984   Cisneros moves to San Antonio, Texas; *The House on Mango Street* is published by Arte Público Press.

1985   *The House on Mango Street* wins the Before Columbus Foundation's American Book Award.

1987   *My Wicked Wicked Ways*, a collection of poetry, is published by Third Woman Press.

1991   *Woman Hollering Creek and Other Stories* is published by Random House.

1992   Cisneros purchases her own home in King William, a historical district in South Antonio, Texas.

1994   *Loose Woman* and *Hairs/Pelitos* are published by Alfred A. Knopf.

1995   Cisneros is awarded the MacArthur Foundation Fellowship.

1997   Cisneros's father, Alfredo Cisneros, dies on February 12; the city of San Antonio takes issue with the purple color Cisneros paints her house.

2002   *Caramelo*, or, *Puro Cuento*, is published by Alfred A. Knopf.

2004   *Vintage Cisneros* is published by Vintage Books.

2007   Cisneros's mother dies on November 1.

2009   Cisneros embarks on a national tour to celebrate the twenty-fifth anniversary of the publication of *The House on Mango Street.*

Chapter 1. Tug of War

1. Don Swaim, "Audio Interview With Sandra Cisneros," *Wired for Books*, 1991, <http://wiredforbooks.org/sandracisneros/> (September 5, 2008).

2. Mary B. W. Tabor, "At the Library With: Sandra Cisneros; A Solo Traveler in Two Worlds," *New York Times*, January 7, 1993, <http://query.nytimes.com/gst/fullpage.html?res= 9FOCEDC 1031F93> (September 5, 2008).

3. "Chicana Novelist and Poet Sandra Cisneros," *Pacifica Radio*, March 3, 1998, <http://www.democracynow.org/1998/3/3/chicana_ novelist_and_poet_sandra_cisneros> (September 5, 2008).

4. Orange County Department of Education, "Sandra Cisneros," *Video Conferencing in Orange County*, October 25, 2005, <http:// webcast.ocde.us/cisneros2.mov> (October 21, 2008).

5. Swaim.

6. Felix Contreras, "Intersections: When Languages Collide," *National Public Radio*, March 11, 2008, <http://www.npr.org/ templates/story/story.php?storyId=1866475> (September 17, 2008).

7. "Chicana Novelist and Poet Sandra Cisneros."

8. Garrison Keillor, "Sandra Cisneros and Joy Harjo," *Literary Friendships From American Public Media, National Public Radio*, 2005, <http://literaryfriendships.publicradio.org> (September 17, 2008).

9. Ibid.

10. Ibid.

11. Ibid.

12. Orange County Department of Education.

13. Ibid.

14. Ibid.

15. Ibid.

16. Ibid.

17. Tabor.

18. "Chicana Novelist and Poet Sandra Cisneros."

19. Denise Chavez with Sandra Cisneros, "Lannon Reading & Conversations," Lannon Video Library, October 11, 2001, <http://www.lannan.org/lf/rc/event/denise-chavez/> (September 23, 2008).

20. "Chicana Novelist and Poet Sandra Cisneros."

21. Ibid.

22. Brendan R. Watson, "Contesting Ethnic Representation and Anglo Cultural Dominance in Contemporary Chicana/o Literature" (senior honors thesis, Washington University, St. Louis, March 19, 2004), <http://smudgedink.org/thesis.pdf> (September 23, 2008).

23. Ibid.

24. Contreras.

Chapter 2. Plot and the Experimental Structure of Vignettes

1. Orange County Department of Education, "Sandra Cisneros," *Video Conferencing in Orange County,* October 25, 2005, <http://webcast.ocde.us/cisneros2.mov> (October 21, 2008).

2. "Chicana Novelist and Poet Sandra Cisneros," *Pacifica Radio,* March 3, 1998, <http://www.democracynow.org/1998/3/3/chi-cana_novelist_and_poet_sandra_cisneros> (September 5, 2008).

3. Peter Trachtenberg, *The House on Mango Street* teacher's guide, *Random House Academic Resources,* 1994, <http://www.randomhouse.com/acmart/teacherguides/houmantg.html> (September 23, 2008).

4. Ibid.

5. Don Swaim, "Audio Interview With Sandra Cisneros," *Wired for Books,* 1991, <http://wiredforbooks.org/sandracisneros/> (September 5, 2008).

6. Orange County Department of Education.

7. Sandra Cisneros, *The House on Mango Street* (New York: Random House, 1984), p. 4.

8. Ibid.

9. Ibid., pp. 23–25.

10. Ibid., pp. 26–27.

11. Ibid., pp. 29–30.

12. Ibid., pp. 79–80.

13. Ibid., pp. 92–93, 94–98, 99–100, 101–102.

14. Ibid., p. 84.

15. Ibid., p. 31.

16. Ibid., p 13.

17. Ibid., p. 28.

18. Ibid., pp. 90–91.

19. Ibid., pp. 31–32.

20. Ibid., pp. 84–85.

21. Ibid., p. 105.

22. Swaim.

Chapter 3. Themes of Embracing Culture and Pushing It Away

1. Sandra Cisneros, *The House on Mango Street* (New York: Random House, 1984), pp. 10–11.

2. Ibid.

3. Orange County Department of Education, "Sandra Cisneros," *Video Conferencing in Orange County*, October 25, 2005, <http://webcast.ocde.us/cisneros2.mov> (October 21, 2008).

4. Felix Contreras, "Intersections: When Languages Collide," *National Public Radio*, March 11, 2008, <http://www.npr.org/templates/story/story.php?storyId=1866475> (September 17, 2008)

5. Cisneros, pp. 62–64.

6. Ibid., pp. 103–106.

7. Contreras.

8. Orange County Department of Education.

9. Peter Trachtenberg, *The House on Mango Street* teacher's guide, *Random House Academic Resources*, 1994, <http://www.randomhouse.com/acmart/teacherguides/houmantg.html> (September 23, 2008).

10. Orange County Department of Education.

11. Stella Bolaki, "'This Bridge We Call Home': Crossing and Bridging Spaces in Sandra Cisneros's *The House on Mango Street*," Borders and Boundaries, *eSharp,* Issue 5, Summer 2005, <http://www.gla.ac.uk/media/media_41166_en.pdf> (September 23, 2008).

12. Cisneros, pp. 41–42.

13. Ibid., pp. 72–73, 94–98.

14. Orange County Department of Education.

Chapter 4. Poetic Devices

1. "*The House on Mango Street:* Themes, Motifs, and Symbols," *SparkNotes,* 2006, <http://www.sparknotes.com/lit/mangostreet/themes.html> (September 23, 2008).

2. Sandra Cisneros, *The House on Mango Street* (New York: Random House, 1984), p. 4.

3. "*The House on Mango Street:* Themes, Motifs, and Symbols."

4. Cisneros, p. 47.

5. "*The House on Mango Street:* Themes, Motifs, and Symbols."

6. Ibid.

7. Maria Elena de Valdes, "In Search of Identity in Cisneros's *The House on Mango Street*," *Canadian Review of American Studies,* Vol. 23, No. 1, Fall 1992, p. 62.

8. Ibid.

Chapter 5. The Character of Esperanza Cordero

1. Ellen C. Mayock, "The Bicultural Construction of Self in Cisneros, Alvarez, and Santiago," *The Bilingual Review/La Revista Belingue,* Vol. 23, No. 3, Fall 1998, pp. 223–229.

2. "*The House on Mango Street* Setting/Characters/Character Descriptions," *TheBestNotes.com,* May 12, 2008, <http://thebestnotes.com/booknotes/House_On_Mango_Street/ House_On_Mango_Street_Cisneros02.html> (September 23, 2008).

3. Mayock, pp. 223–229.

4. Ibid., p. 227.

Chapter 6. The Corderos' World—Culture, Class, and Stereotypes

1. Gayle Elliott, "An Interview With Sandra Cisneros," *Missouri Review*, Vol. 25, November 1, 2002, <http://moreview.com/content/dynamic/view_text.php?text_id=1093> (September 23, 2008).

2. Maria Elena de Valdes, "In Search of Identity in Cisneros's *The House on Mango Street*," *Canadian Review of American Studies*, Vol. 23, No. 1, Fall 1992, p. 56.

3. Sandra Cisneros, *The House on Mango Street* (New York: Random House, 1984), p. 6.

4. Ibid., p. 8.

5. Ibid., pp. 56–57.

6. Ibid., pp. 90–91.

7. Ibid., p. 88.

8. Ellen C. Mayock, "The Bicultural Contruction of Self in Cisneros, Alvarez, and Santiago," *The Bilingual Review/La Revista Belingue*, Vol. 23, No. 3, Fall 1998, p. 225.

Chapter 7. Other Works

1. Maria Newman, "Sandra Cisneros: Her New Book, Her New Look," *Hispanic*, September 2002, p. 45.

2. "Hispanic Heritage: Biographies: Sandra Cisneros," *Gale Cengage Learning*, n.d., <http://www.galegroup.com/free_resources/chh/bio/cisneros_s.htm> (October 21, 2008).

3. Jim Sagel, "Sandra Cisneros: Conveying the Riches of the Latin American Culture Is the Author's Literary Goal," *Publishers Weekly*, Vol. 238, No. 15, March 29, 1991, p. 74, <http://www.lasmujeres.com/sandracisneros/sisnerosgoal.shtml> (September 23, 2008).

4. "A Conversation With Sandra Cisneros," *Miambiance*, Vol. 13, n.d., <http://www.mdc.edu/kendall/miambiancemagazine/issue13/interview.html> (September 23, 2008).

5. Newman, p. 44.

6. Ibid.

7. "Major Works," *SandraCisneros.com,* n.d., <http://www. sandracisneros.com/major_works.php> (September 23, 2008).

8. Ana Caban, "'Mango Street' Ripens Into Lyrical Literary Success," *Milwaukee Journal Sentinel,* October 11, 2003, <http://www.jsonline.com/story/index.aspx?id=176182> (September 23, 2008).

9. "Major Works," *SandraCisneros.com.*

10. Barbara Hoffert, *Library Journal,* January 15, 2007, <http://www.libraryjournal.com/article/CA6403915.html> (September 23, 2008).

11. Ibid.

12. Ibid.

13. "Major Works," *SandraCisneros.com.*

14. Laurel Darrow, "Celebrating Female Love and Lust," *Seattle Times,* Entertainment and Arts, July 13, 1994, <http://community. seattletimes.nwsource.com/archive/?date=19940703&sl ug=1918598> (October 21, 2008).

15. Ellen McCracken, "Postmodern Ethnicity in Sandra Cisneros's *Caramelo*: Hybridity, Spectacle, and Memory in the Nomadic Text," *Journal of American Studies of Turkey,* No. 12, Fall 2000, <http://www.bilkent.edu.tr/~jast/Number12/McCracken.htm#_ ftn4> (September 23, 2008).

16. Ibid.

17. *Hairs/Pelitos* by Sandra Cisneros, *Amazon.com,* n.d., <http:// www.amazon.com/gp/product/product-description/0679890076/ ref=dp_proddesc_0?ie =UTF8&n=283155&s=books> (September 23, 2008).

18. Gayle Elliott, "An Interview With Sandra Cisneros," *Missouri Review,* Vol. 25, November 1, 2002, <http://moreview.com/ content/dynamic/view_text.php?text_id=1093> (September 23, 2008).

19. "Major Works," *SandraCisneros.com.*

20. Ibid.

21. Elliott.

22. Wanda Sabit, "Author Sandra Cisneros Shares Her Marriage With Writing," *Berkeley Daily Planet,* October 31, 2001, <http://www.berkeleydailyplanet.com/issue/2001-10-31/article/7953> (September 23, 2008).

23. Newman, p. 44.

24. Ibid.

25. "Major Works," *SandraCisneros.com.*

26. Keir Graff, review of *Caramelo,* by Sandra Cisneros, *Booklist: American Library Association,* August 1, 2002, p. 1883.

27. Margaret Randall, "Weaving a Spell," *Women's Review of Books,* October 2002, <http://www.wellesley.edu/WomensReview/archive/2002/10/highlt.html#randall> (September 23, 2008).

28. Ibid.

29. Ibid.

30. Newman, p. 45.

31. Ibid., p. 46.

32. Elliott.

33. Newman, p. 47.

34. Vivianne Schnitzer, "Hispanic Heritage Month Keynote: Author Sandra Cisneros Explores Complexity of Latina Identity," *University Record Online,* September 25, 2006, <http://www.ur.umich.edu/0607/Sept25_06/19.shtml> (September 23, 2008).

Chapter 8. The Importance of This Work

1. Margaret Randall, "Weaving a Spell," *Women's Review of Books,* October 2002, <http://www.wellesley.edu/WomensReview/archive/2002/10/highlt.html#randall> (September 23, 2008).

2. Ana Caban, "'Mango Street' Ripens Into Lyrical Literary Success," *Milwaukee Journal Sentinel,* October 11, 2003, <http://www.jsonline.com/story/index.aspx?id=176182> (September 23, 2008).

3. Ibid.

4. Maria Newman, "Sandra Cisneros: Her New Book, Her New Look," *Hispanic,* September 2002, p. 44.

5. "MacArthur Fellows: C," *MacArthur Foundation,* n.d., <http://www.macfound.org/site/c.lkLXJ8MQKrH/b.1139461/k.9375/Fellows_List__C.htm> (September 23, 2008).

6. Mireya Navarro, "Telling a Tale of Immigrants Whose Stories Go Untold," *New York Times,* November 12, 2002, <http://query.nytimes.com/gst/fullpage.html?res=9900E3D71331F931A25752C1A9649C8B63&sec=&spon=&pagewanted=1> (September 23, 2008).

7. Leslie Averback, "Promoting Adolescent Voice Through Latina Literature," *Child and Adolescent Social Work Journal,* Vol. 15, No. 5, October 1998, pp. 379–389.

8. Ibid.

9. Ellen C. Mayock, "The Bicultural Construction of Self in Cisneros, Alvarez, and Santiago," *The Bilingual Review/La Revista Belingue,* Vol. 23, No. 3, Fall 1998, p. 239.

10. Carole A. Poppleton, "Sandra Cisneros's *The House on Mango Street*: Experiencing Poetical Prose," essay and lesson plan, *The InternetTESL Journal,* Vol. 5, No. 10, October 1999, <http://iteslj.org/Lessons/Poppleton-MangoStreet.html> (September 23, 2008).

11. Jim Sagel, "Sandra Cisneros: Conveying the Riches of the Latin American Culture Is the Author's Literary Goal," *Publishers Weekly,* Vol. 238, No. 15, March 29, 1991, p. 74, <http://www.lasmujeres.com/sandracisneros/sisnerosgoal.shtml> (September 23, 2008).

12. Kathleen J. Ryan, "Teaching *The House on Mango Street*: Engaging Race, Class, and Gender in a White Classroom," *The Free Library,* December 22, 2002, <http://www.thefreelibrary.com/Teaching+'The+House+on+Mango+Street':+engaging+race,+class,+and...-a097725112> (September 23, 2008).

13. Gayle Elliott, "An Interview With Sandra Cisneros," *Missouri Review,* Vol. 25, November 1, 2002, <http://moreview.com/content/dynamic/view_text.php?text_id=1093> (September 23, 2008).

14. Ellen McCracken, "Postmodern Ethnicity in Sandra Cisneros's *Caramelo*: Hybridity, Spectacle, and Memory in the Nomadic Text," *Journal of American Studies of Turkey*, No. 12, Fall 2000, <http://www.bilkent.edu.tr/~jast/Number12/McCracken.htm#_ftn4> (September 23, 2008).

15. Maria-Antonia Oliver-Rotger, "An Interview With Sandra Cisneros," *Voices*, May 14, 2005, <http://voices.cla.umn.edu/vg/interviews/vg_interviews/cisneros_sandra.html> (October 16, 2008).

16. Jen Buckendorff, "Father's Death Opened New Insights for 'Caramelo' Author Sandra Cisneros," *Seattle Times*, October 21, 2003, <http://community.seattletimes.nwsource.com/ archive/?date=20031021&slug=cisneros21> (September 23, 2008).

17. Ibid.

18. Ibid.

19. Darryl Fears, "Hispanic or Latino? Debate Stirs Pride, Emotion," *Seattle Times*, August 26, 2003, <http://archives.seattletimes.nwsource.com/archive/?date=20030826&slug=hispanic26> (September 23, 2008).

20. Ibid.

21. Ibid.

22. Ibid.

23. Ibid.

24. Mary B. W. Tabor, "At the Library With: Sandra Cisneros; A Solo Traveler in Two Worlds," *New York Times*, January 7, 1993, <http://query.nytimes.com/gst/fullpage.html?res= 9FOCEDC 1031F93> (September 5, 2008).

25. Buckendorff.

Chapter 9. Best-Seller Lists and Awards

1. "Alfredo Cisneros Del Moral Foundation," *SandraCisneros.com*, n.d., <http://www.sandracisneros.com/foundation.php> (September 23, 2008).

2. Ibid.

3. Ibid.

4. Ibid.

5. "Elvira Cisneros," *SandraCisneros.com*, June 4, 2008, <http://www.sandracisneros.com/2007-11-01_elvira_cisneros.php> (October 22, 2008).

6. Ibid.

7. "Macondo Libre' Events Benefit Foundation," *SandraCisneros. com*, June 4, 2008, <http://www.sandracisneros.com/2007-06-06_ macondo_libre.php> (October 22, 2008).

8. Ibid.

9. "About Sandra Cisneros," *SandraCisneros.com*, June 4, 2008, <http://www.sandracisneros.com/bio.php> (October 22, 2008).

10. Ibid.

card catalog—A file cabinet that pre-dates computers as the resource to list books in a library.

Chicano/a—A term used to describe Mexican-American people. Men are traditionally referred to as Chicano or Latino and women are referred to as Chicana or Latina.

chingones—A slang term referring to men who behave with machismo.

ethnicity—A particular affiliation or group.

gender—Traits typically associated with a specific sexual group, either male or female.

machismo—Behaving with bravado.

metaphor—A figure of speech in which one object or idea is denoted by a different object or idea.

taboo—Banned on grounds of immorality, taste, or because it is considered dangerous.

vignette—A short descriptive literary scene.

MAJOR WORKS
BY SANDRA CISNEROS

1980   *Bad Boys*

1984   *The House on Mango Street*

1987   *My Wicked Wicked Ways*

1991   *Woman Hollering Creek and Other Stories*

1994   *La Casa en Mango Street* (Spanish translation of *The House on Mango Street*)

        Loose Woman

        Hairs/Pelitos

2002   *Caramelo, or, Puro Cuento*

2004   *Vintage Cisneros*

Carlson, Lori M. *Cool Salsa: Bilingual Poems on Growing Up Latino in the United States.* New York: H. Holt and Company, 2008.

Carlson, Lori M., Flavio Marais, and Manuel River-Ortez. *Voices in First Person: Reflections on Latino Identity.* New York: Atheneum, 2008.

Garcia, Cristina, ed. *Bordering Fires: The Vintage Book of Contemporary Mexican and Chicano/a Literature.* New York: Vintage Books, 2006.

Sandra Cisneros's "Once Again I Prove the Theory of Relativity": A Study Guide from Gale's "Poetry for Students" (Volume 19, Chapter 8) [Digital].

Stavans, Ilan. *Latina Writers.* Westport, Conn.: Greenwood Press, 2008.

Sandra Cisneros's Official Web site

http://www.sandracisneros.com

Sandra Cisneros Biography, *Modern American Poetry,* **University of Illinois**

http://www.english.uiuc.edu/maps/poets/a_f/cisneros/cisneros.htm

Macondo Foundation, Inc.

http://www.macondoworkshop.org

INDEX

Activism, 70, 82, 93, 97–98
Alfredo Cisneros Del Moral
    Foundation, 102–104
Alicia, 35, 36, 58
Alvarez, Julia, 25
American Book Award, 85
Arte Público Press, 23, 38, 63
"A Smart Cookie," 36
awards/honors
    overview, 99–107

Bad Boys, 18, 63
barrios, 56, 67, 92–93, 97
Before Columbus Foundation, 85
Bergholz, Susan, 65
"Boys and Girls," 32

California State University, 66
Caramelo (Puro Cuento), 24, 65–66, 68,
    76–81, 84, 99, 101–102
"Cathy Queen of Cats," 35
Cervantes, Lorna Dee, 18
"Chanclas," 52
change, creating, 23, 48
chapbooks, 18
Chicano Renaissance, 25
Cisneros, Alfredo, 11, 13, 20, 76–77,
    94–95, 103
Cisneros, Elvira "Vera," 36, 104–105
Cisneros, Sandra
    childhood/family life, 5–12
    education, 8–9, 13–18
class issues, 9–10, 14–16, 59–62, 80,
    90–92
Cordoza, Esperanza. See also themes.
    development of, 18–20, 28
    identity struggle, 6, 18–19, 22,
        29–32, 37, 40–41, 60
    portrayal of, 55–58
culture, 20, 25, 57–62, 90–92

Depression, 64–66
Dove, Rita, 15

"**E**lenita, Cards, Palm Water," 42
Elvira Cordero Cisneros Scholarship
    Fund, 105
ethnicity, 92

Feminism, 19, 75
"Four Skinny Trees," 51

Grandmothers, 78, 81–82

"**H**airs," 60
Hairs/Pelitos, 24, 72
Harjo, Joy, 15
Hispanics, 96, 97
home painting controversy, 70–72
House on Mango Street, The
    as autobiography, 11–12, 19
    awards, 85
    character portrayal in, 32–35, 41–42
    importance of, 85–98
    inspiration for, 15–19, 22, 27–28, 41
    poetic devices, 49–54
    publishing of, 23, 63, 84
    reviews, 38, 63–64
    sales, 62
    storyline, 31–37
    structure, 28–31
    themes (See themes)
    translation of, 85
    writing process, 21–23, 48, 63
    writing techniques, 25, 39–41, 42–45

Immigration, 82
Infinito, 107
Iowa Writers Workshop, 14–18, 92

Labels, 96

language as device, 17, 25, 30, 42–45, 67–70, 79, 80, 84, 86, 90–91

Latinos, 96

"Linoleum Roses," 34

Loose Woman, 24, 68–70, 84, 100

"Louie, His Cousin and His Other Cousin," 32

Loyola university, 13, 101

Lucha Libre, 106

Macarthur Foundation Fellowship, 87, 95, 100–101

Macondo Foundation, 102, 105, 106

Mango Press, 63

"Marin," 32–33, 57

metaphors, 49–53

"Mexican Hat Dance," 17–18

Minerva, 34–37, 50

"Minerva Writes Poems," 36–37

"My Lucy Friend Who Smells Like Corn," 74

"My Name," 29, 40–41

My Wicked Wicked Ways, 24, 64, 67, 84

National Endowment of the Arts grants, 22–23, 63, 66, 101

Nenny, 32, 53, 61

"Never Marry a Mexican," 75

"No Speak English," 45

Nuestro magazine, 17–18

One Book, One Community programs, 87, 99

Paz, Octavio, 25

privilege, 9–10, 14–16, 59–62, 80, 90, 91

Quotation marks, 43–44

Racism, 16–17, 35, 92

Rafaela, 33, 45, 50

"Rafaela Drinks Coconut and Papaya Juice on Tuesdays," 33, 45

Random House, 65

"Red Clowns," 34

reviews, 38, 63–64, 67–69, 72–74, 79–81

rhymes, 53

risk taking, 32

Sally, 33–34, 47, 50, 52, 58

shoes, 51–52

Soto, Gary, 18

stereotypes, 25, 59–62, 70, 90–91

Teaching, 19–21, 63, 66, 98

"The Family of Little Feet," 30, 46, 51

themes

autonomy, 46–47, 51–54, 58, 62

bicultural world, 42–43, 58

confinement, 33, 45–46, 49–50

differences, 60–61

feminism, 19

gender roles, 32–36, 45–50, 57–58, 61

home, 42, 57–58

identity struggle, 6, 18–19, 22, 29–32, 37, 40–41, 60

love/family, 59–61

overview, 28

perseverance, 51

powerlessness, 32–36, 45–50, 57–58, 61

racism, 35

sexuality, 30, 34, 46–47

shame, 36, 52, 61

truth, search for, 28

women, abuse of, 21–22, 25, 33–34, 47–48, 57–58

"There Was an Old Woman She Had So Many Children She Didn't Know What to Do," 33

"Those Who Don't," 35

tours, 85–86, 105–107

traditions, 20, 25, 57–62, 90–92

trees, 51

Vargas, Rose, 33

vignettes, 28–29

Vintage Books, 84

Vintage Cisneros, 84

Virgin of Guadalupe, 82–84

Weaving, 39–40

windows, 49–50

Woman Hollering Creek and Other Stories, 24, 73–76, 95, 99–100

women, abuse of, 21–22, 25, 33–34, 47–48, 57–58

writing

    influences on, 12, 41

    inspirations, 12–17, 21–22

    language as device, 17, 25, 30, 42–45, 67–70, 79, 80, 84, 86, 90–91

    motivations, 23, 48

    poetic devices, 49–54

    process, 21–23, 48, 63

    techniques, 25, 39–41, 42–45

Writing in My Pajamas, 84, 107

About the Author

Ann Angel has written many young adult books that include biographies for educational markets. She has also written fiction ever since the publication of her first middle grade novel, *Real for Sure Sister.* She obtained her MFA at Vermont College and most recently created *Such A Pretty Face,* a collection of short stories about alternative perspectives of beauty by new and known writers.